Test your

# Personality

## GENE CROZIER

Series editors: GARETH LEWIS & GENE CROZIER

## Hodder & Stoughton

A MEMBER OF THE HODDER HEADLINE GROUP

the Institute
of Management

The Institute of Management (IM) is the leading
organisation for professional management. Its purpose is
to promote the art and science of management in every
sector and at every level, through research, education,
training and development, and representation of
members' views on management issues.

This series is commissioned by IM Enterprises Limited,
a subsidiary of the Institute of Management, providing
commercial services.

**Management House,**
**Cottingham Road,**
**Corby,**
**Northants NN17 1TT**
**Tel: 01536 204222;**
**Fax: 01536 201651**
**Website: http://www.inst-mgt.org.uk**

Registered in England no 3834492
Registered office: 2 Savoy Court, Strand,
London WC2R 0EZ

Orders: please contact Bookpoint Ltd, 39 Milton Park, Abingdon, Oxon OX14
4TD.
Telephone: (44) 01235 400414, Fax: (44) 01235 400454. Lines are open from 9.00
– 6.00, Monday to Saturday, with a 24 hour message answering service.
Email address: orders@bookpoint.co.uk

*British Library Cataloguing in Publication Data*
A catalogue record for this title is available from The British Library

ISBN 0 340 78006 1

First published 2000
Impression number    10 9 8 7 6 5 4 3 2 1
Year                 2004 2003 2002 2001 2000

Typeset by Fakenham Photosetting Limited, Fakenham, Norfolk.
Printed in Great Britain for Hodder & Stoughton Education, a division of
Hodder Headline Plc, 338 Euston Road, London NW1 3BH by Cox & Wyman
Ltd, Reading, Berkshire.

# Contents

# Introduction

The 'Test Yourself' series covers a wide range of skills, competencies, capabilities and styles that contribute to our uniqueness as individuals and our performance in the workplace. Some of these qualities can be measured by objective tests that we call psychometric tests. Others of these skills are assessed or evaluated using a variety of other methods.

The use of psychometric or psychological tests has grown enormously in the last few decades, so much so that if you apply for a job in a medium to large organisation, the chances are three to one that you will be required to take a psychometric test at some stage during the selection process. The tests that are used fall into two major groups. The first of these focuses on aspects of maximum performance. These are tests of aptitude and ability, which are the subject of another book in the series. The other group of tests, personality tests or personality questionnaires, focuses on aspects of our preferences, style and developed habits.

This second group – the subject of this book – is important for a number of reasons:

- When part of a carefully designed selection and recruitment process, these tests can identify the probable link between the nature of a particular job and our natural preferences.
- They can provide us with a powerful development tool.

- People often fear these tests because they feel they may reveal something negative about their personality.

This last point is important. This fear is usually based on a lack of knowledge of how such tests are designed and what they measure.

This book is designed to explain and reassure. We will set out what it is exactly that these tests measure, and how this is done. We will also describe some of the most commonly used tests, how they fit in with the repertoire of other kinds of test and what use is made of the information. We will give you a chance to 'have a go' and to get a good idea of your own personality. Finally, we will explain how personality tests can be used to maximise your potential.

The chapters in this book follow the following sequence:

- The background to personality testing
- The nature of personality
- The main types of personality test
- Preparing yourself for personality tests
- Test yourself
- Where to go next

# The background to personality testing

In this first chapter, we shall examine the background to personality testing and its importance. That it is increasingly seen as important is evidenced by the substantial growth in the use of personality questionnaires in recent times.

To do this we will consider:

- What are personality tests?
- Why are personality tests important?
- New approaches to management
- Personal effectiveness and development

## What are personality tests?

One of the most important changes in society over the last 50 years has been the growing impact of psychology on our lives. In every walk of life, the importance of an individual's personal qualities, attitudes, skills and experience in influencing the way they interact with others is increasingly recognised. We all know that successful marketing campaigns are designed to press the right 'psychological' buttons in the population and we are much more open to discussing the role of personality in the workplace.

Matching this growth, there has also been an explosion in the use of psychological or psychometric tests. There are now literally hundreds of publishing houses selling thousands of psychometric tests in every different shape and form. Just one of these questionnaires sells millions of copies every year, so testing is big business. People often equate 'psychometric' or 'psychological' tests with 'personality' tests, but in fact psychometric tests include a much wider range of tests than personality tests. So, what is the difference between the two and how do we recognise them?

## What is a psychometric test?

Finding a good definition of a psychometric test is not that easy. The British Psychological Society offers the following: 'an instrument designed to produce a quantitative assessment of some psychological attribute or attributes.'

'Some psychological attribute' gives us a lot of freedom to interpret the phrase, but certainly doesn't shed too much light on the subject.

Put in a different way, it is a device or test (commonly, but not necessarily, a questionnaire) that provides measurements of any aspect of our psychology – ie thinking or behaviour – that can be measured.

In general, they tend to relate to two distinct (but overlapping) kinds of performance.

*Maximum performance*

Maximum performance tests measure our potential or ability to do certain things. They include tests of intelligence, aptitude or ability. These tests are dealt with in another book in the series, but for now, it is worth noting that they typically:

- have right and wrong answers
- measure the ability or achievement under strict conditions
- involve a level of difficulty so that performance can be compared person to person.

*Habitual performance*

This is also sometimes called *typical performance*, and such tests measure characteristic ways of behaving and how we perceive the world, our attitudes, values and interests. Typically they:

- are self-descriptive
- indicate most typical behaviour or preferences
- don't involve right or wrong answers.

These are the tests that are often referred to as psychological tests or personality tests.

*What puts the 'metric' in psychometric?*

Clearly, as the name implies, this has something to do with measurement. It is primarily the fact that we measure and quantify attributes that distinguishes psychometric testing from subjective judgement. However, developing a test is a whole process, and this involves a number of components.

So there are a number of criteria that enable us to classify a test as psychometric. These include:

- It is constructed according to psychometric principles.
- It is administered in a standardised way.
- It is scored in a standardised way.
- It is interpreted in a standardised way.

## Test construction

As most tests are of the pencil and paper type, they consist of questions or *items* as they are often called. The basic process of constructing a test involves:

1 *generating* a large number of items
2 *piloting and selection of items*, using a number of specialised statistical tests
3 *standardising the scores*, to convert raw scores from the test into a form that allows you to compare an individual with the rest of the population
4 *writing the technical manual*, to provide guidance to users of the tests with information about the relevant statistics, and the appropriate administration and scoring and interpreting of the test.

## Generating items for tests

A personality test is simply a series of questions that assess an individual's thinking, feeling and acting in different situations. For personality tests, there are a number of possibilities:

- *Dual response* – requiring a YES/NO or TRUE/FALSE answer, although a third interim category can be added, eg; YES/NOT SURE/NO, MOSTLY/SOMETIMES/ NEVER, TRUE/NOT SURE/FALSE, AGREE/?/DISAGREE. For example:
  I have never told a lie      TRUE/FALSE
- *Rating scales* – requiring you to say how much you agree or disagree with a statement on a five-point scale. For example:
  I think personality tests are a load of nonsense

| strongly agree | agree | not sure | disagree | strongly disagree |
|---|---|---|---|---|
| ❏ | ❏ | ❏ | ❏ | ❏ |

- **_Forced choice_** – sometimes called ipsative, here requiring you to choose (usually from a pair of words) the most applicable to them. For example:
  When relaxing I would prefer to
  (a) listen to some classical music
  (b) go and play a game of squash (select option a or b).

A key feature of these tests is that they measure your stated preferences (often referred to as self reports). There is no question that they are trying to uncover some hidden part of your nature you would rather cover over. In this respect they are quite different from the use of handwriting tests, where a single interpreter seeks to identify 'hidden' aspects of your personality from a sample of handwriting.

## Selecting and testing items

A lot of work goes into designing and testing personality questionnaires. Typically test designers produce a very large number of questions in the early stages of test design and then reduce and refine the set of questions by subjecting them to an extensive set of statistical tests. This is the most important stage of test design because it needs to show that the test actually measures what it says it does and reliably. It is also the most technical part of test construction and often ignored by test users, on the basis that the hard work and the arithmetic has been done by the test constructor. This is a pity because not all tests are as impressive in achieving their aims as the publishers would like everyone to think.

Here we will just provide a brief overview of the approach, which involves two main concepts:

- validity
- reliability.

*Validity*

A test is valid if it measures what it says it measures. This is a simple starting point, but validity can be a complex topic. There are a number of facets to it, and thus a number of different ways of describing, measuring and demonstrating validity. The most important are:

- **Face validity** – this is the extent to which the test appears to the user to test the attribute in question. Its main value is in gaining cooperation from test-takers.
- **Construct validity** – the question here is whether the test fully describes the attribute being measured.
- **Content validity** – answers the question 'does this test measure all aspects of the attribute in question?'
- **Criterion-related validity** – this establishes the predictive value of the test – whether it can predict some measured, real world criterion. In general, this is quite difficult to achieve to a high degree. However, where it can be justified, it is obviously very powerful.

*Reliability*

Reliability has two distinct meanings. A test is reliable if it is self-consistent, that is, its various parts are measuring the same thing.

A good test should also give the same score for each subject (as long as they have not changed) when they are retested. This is called test-retest reliability.

Reliability is also important as it in turn effects the validity, ie in practice, valid tests are consistent.

## Administering tests

The results of tests are meaningful and reliable only if everyone takes the test in the same conditions. This can be illustrated by a very simple example. Suppose you want to test a group of people using a personality questionnaire. You could just hand the test out and ask the subjects to return it in the next few days. However, there would be a few disadvantages to this:

- They might have different interpretations of the instructions and might fill in the questionnaire incorrectly.
- They might ask their friends about the answers or even get them to take the test.
- They would be doing the test under different conditions.
- They would take differing amounts of time to do the test.

In most personality questionnaires, time is not an issue but if any of the other points apply, we would not truly be able to compare the results from different individuals reliably.

To avoid these problems, test suppliers usually supply a user manual that describes the test administration in some detail, including the actual script to be spoken. This increases the impression of 'sitting an examination' among test-takers, but is there to ensure consistency.

## Interpreting test results

As you shall see later in a trial questionnaire, each question in a test is allocated to a particular characteristic. Each response is scored and all the results for each characteristic are added up at the end. A very simple test for social boldness might contain twenty questions with a TRUE or FALSE answer. The number of TRUE responses would give an indication of social boldness.

If an individual scores 15 out of a maximum of 20 on the test, what does this actually mean? Not a lot, unless it is compared to the way in which other people respond. For this reason, raw scores on a test are always converted to a 'profile score', which compares the individual score with the scores of a known group of people. This process is called standardising the scores.

It works like this:

Like most variables that occur in the natural world, measurements for a population are distributed in a characteristic way. For instance, if we measured the heights of a large and representative sample of the population, and put the heights on a frequency diagram, they would look like this.

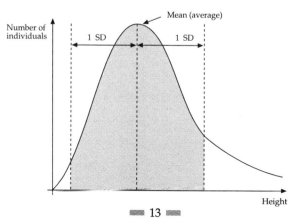

The shape of this line occurs so often in nature that we give it an official name, the normal distribution. It is bell-shaped and symmetrical, and the average (or mean) is the highest point on the curve.

Another statistic that is very relevant in this distribution is called the standard deviation and it measures the spread of values in the distribution. It allows us to quantify the number of people in a test who score above or below particular values.

For example, we know that 68% of people will score between plus and minus 1 SD score (the area shown on the diagram). When raw scores are converted to standardised scores, it places the score in relation to the rest of the population. There are two popular ways of doing this:

1  *Sten (standard ten) scores*. These 'carve' the distribution up into ten units, with the middle being at 5.5.

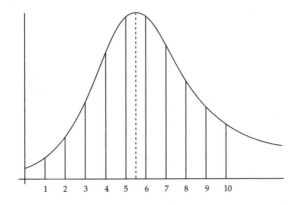

2 *Percentiles*. These carve the distribution up into 100 units, with the middle being 50.

It is, of course, vitally important when working with standardised scores to know the group or population used to produce the questionnaire scores. On most test reports you will find a comment that tells you where the *norms* were obtained from. A percentile score of 60 (which means scores higher than 60% of the population) on an ability test is one thing if you are compared with the population as a whole. However, if you are being compared to a graduate population, or a senior management population, then the interpretation will be slightly different.

## Why are personality tests important?

It is fairly natural to make judgements about the behaviour or potential of other people. If you just think of those people who will have made judgements about you over the years, your list might include parents and relatives, friends, teachers, doctors, colleagues at work, managers and potential employers.

In some cases, the judgements will have had a pretty significant effect on your career. If you manage other people, you will often be called to provide assessments that will impact on their working lives. For example:

- Are they suitable for promotion?
- Will they perform well in a particular role or job?
- How well do they get on with other people?
- Are they in line with company policy and values?

These are important questions, but often these judgements will have been subjective or based on flawed or incomplete information. If we think about our own experience, we can probably identify many instances where we were less than convinced about the quality of decisions made on our behalf.

In the fields of clinical and educational psychology, the issues are too important to leave to chance. The diagnosis of psychological or educational difficulties early enough to allow effective treatment was one of the major drivers behind the development of psychometric testing. The first person to have taken a more systematic or 'scientific' approach to measuring some aspect of human behaviour or capability was a French psychologist called Binet, who was interested in the differences between children that affected educational performance. The focus of his interest was in those skills, judgement, comprehension and ability to reason which he felt distinguished achievers and non-achievers. He invented the term 'intelligence quotient' (IQ) to describe these characteristics, and he went on to develop a test to measure them objectively.

The first major users of such tests were the military in the USA, but since the Second World War psychometric testing has moved both to education and to organisational life in general. The main difference is that we can now measure a much broader range of characteristics using a comprehensive range of sophisticated instruments.

## Selection and recruitment

One of the key areas of growth in the use of psychometric tests in organisations has been in selection and recruitment.

If you apply for a job in a larger organisation or use a selection and recruitment agency for career development, then you can expect to be required to take some form of test and probably both for aptitude and ability as well as personality. Why is this so? Well, for most of our working lives, the curriculum vitae along with the interview has been the stock-in-trade procedure for selection. Yet there is a wealth of evidence demonstrating that it is flawed. It has been shown, for example, that:

- Interviewers make up their mind about a candidate from first impressions and then seek to justify that judgement.
- Judgements are often based on less than rational grounds like appearance, gender, accents etc.
- Few interviewers have appropriate training or skills for the job.
- Even well-conducted interviews are only 25% better than choosing someone by sticking a pin in a list of candidates (BPS).

So what we see in practice are decisions based on a collection of first impressions, negative information, self-delusion by interviewers and stereotyping. All of these limitations stem from the fact that interviewers base their decisions on data that is almost entirely subjective.

Recognition that many selection processes are flawed has led HR professionals to identify more rational and effective ways to carry out selection. One good incentive for this is to avoid the cost of getting it wrong. Many costing exercises have been done, and, of course, it differs according to circumstances. However, even for a middle manager, a poor appointment can cost upwards of

£100,000 when the indirect as well as the direct costs are taken into account.

This means quite clearly that it is significantly cheaper to do it right the first time and every time, even if the costs of selection are higher. Psychometric testing has an important role to play in good selection procedures and can greatly increase the chances of success.

Aptitude and ability tests can be linked to the *job description*, which has been designed though a comprehensive job analysis. Personality questionnaires can then provide insight into the degree of fit between an individual and the *person specification* implied by the job specification. This topic will be discussed in greater detail in Chapter 4.

## New approaches to management

There are many others reasons why personality testing has grown in recent years. Since the 1930s there has been a global move away from the scientific approach to management towards a more obvious human relations approach to management. We have developed a deeper understanding of the fact that the motivation of workers is a key factor in their productivity at work. Organisations now have to work much harder to retain skilled staff and we now take it for granted that investment in people is as important as investment in other aspects of business or organisational life.

Nevertheless, personality testing has only really exploded in recent years, so there must be other influences that have stimulated this growth. The broader influences on organisations that have probably been important revolve around the increasing volatility of the job market. They include:

- pressure for improved competitiveness
- downsizing and extensive change programmes
- increased focus on productivity and therefore performance measurement
- increased focus on creativity and teambuilding, and thus on personal behaviour and skills.

Organisational priorities are changing. This is the information age and the knowledge economy. We will surely see an acceleration of the growing importance of the skills, capabilities and knowledge that people hold, and for many organisations it will be the most important or their only asset. Protecting intellectual capital in the form of acquired knowledge and people can only been achieved if you know what you have.

Psychometric tests (both aptitude/ability and personality) have been able to provide some answers to these issues. Some of the factors that have encouraged increased uptake include:

1  an improved professionalisation of the HR function in organisations
2  a greater awareness of the importance of personal skills in job performance, and the influence of personal behaviour preferences on this
3  increased mobility in the job market, linked to a greater awareness of the cost of making the wrong appointment, has led to a search for more 'intelligent' tools to assess people for recruitment purposes

4   testing itself has become more sophisticated with many
    more tests and suppliers of tests within the market
5   a substantial increase in the priority of learning and
    development in many organisations; this includes a
    greater need to assess people in terms of strengths,
    weaknesses and development needs
6   a movement toward assessment as part of performance
    management
7   changes in the 'contract' between organisation and
    employee that encompass much more than just the
    exchange of labour for money
8   improved awareness of human resource management
    issues in quality frameworks, such as the UK's *Investors
    In People* initiative
9   the rise of competence-based development schemes.

## Personal effectiveness – and development

Increasingly, we see a greater dialogue between employers
and employees in their joint search for success. Social
contracts between the two are becoming increasingly
sophisticated as organisations seek to combine strategic
direction with performance management, employee
incentive and reward schemes, training and development
(and even what are often called employment release
schemes) within a single integrated framework. Individuals
increasingly are able to place their personal aspirations and
agendas high on the list of issues when talking to their
employers.

The issues involved are complex and people need a
common language and models to move forward. This
explains why the competency movement has found such

favour in many organisations. Organisations are increasingly using the notion of competence as a language to describe the skills that underwrite their organisational development. The particular blend of skills, knowledge, qualities and attitudes that go towards excellent performance at work are often explicitly called competencies, but are also referred to as personal effectiveness.

Although there is no such thing as a good or bad personality profile, there is a good or bad match between our profile and our job. This 'closeness of fit' between our personality and the nature of the environment is an important aspect of our lives and one which is unfortunately not given enough attention in many organisations.

Some of the 'core' skills of personal effectiveness which seem to be most sought after include:

- teamworking
- leadership
- interpersonal skills
- management skills
- managing change
- customer skills
- managing self
- lifelong learning and development.

In all of these areas, an understanding of how our personality contributes to success will be vital but will need to be linked to improved ways of assessing these skills. Psychometric testing offers one such solution, so we can expect further growth in the use of the tests, especially since there is still much unexploited potential for the further development of instruments and processes to support organisational and personality development.

Unfortunately, there are still many barriers to self-analysis in some organisations, for example:

- Organisations sometimes actively discourage any form of reflective thinking that might be described as 'contemplating your navel'.
- Many managers are conditioned to presenting an image of the confident, organised decision-maker and are unwilling to discuss any issues that might be thought of as weaknesses.
- The personality profiles of many managers make them less likely to want to analyse themselves carefully.

We hope this guide will encourage you to consider ways of developing your personality in the future.

## Summary

- There are two types of psychometric test – aptitude/ability tests and personality tests.
- The 'science' of testing means that not only are tests systematically designed, but test designers need to pay attention to issues of reliability and validity.
- Tests should be administered and scored in a standardised way following strict instructions.

- Scores are made meaningful by converting them to standardised scores, which compare a result with some population. The most usual ways to do this are by using sten scores or percentiles.
- Although personality tests are commonly used in selection and recruitment, changes in the workplace are emphasising the contribution of personal skills to success. Personality tests provide a valuable tool in maximising performance.

In the next chapter, we will review the nature of personality and the theoretical basis on which most personality questionnaires are based.

# The nature of personality

## What is personality?

So far we have examined the purpose of personality tests and the way in which they are designed and validated. Before we review some of the main types and provide you with an opportunity to test yourself, we shall spend some time on studying the nature of personality.

Ask 20 psychologists to define personality and you will get twenty different answers. What they generally mention is an individual's characteristic patterns of thinking, feeling and acting across a wide range of situations. In other words, what are the consistent features of the way they behave? What makes them unique? Already here we have the concept of consistency and repetition (ie it can be measured).

## The development of modern personality theory

Interest in measuring an individual's psychology can be traced back to the Second World War, when the need to recruit large numbers of men into the armed forces led to the development of mental aptitude tests in the USA and Britain. Personality testing really did not get off the ground until after the war, although the theory behind these tests was developed by Allport in the 1930s.

The growth of personality testing can be linked directly to the development of electronic computers, allowing researchers to calculate complex statistics on large samples with many variables. Up until this time, the calculations required to study behaviour statistically were just too large.

Research into the nature of personality has mainly focused on an emphasis on personality traits and on typologies.

## Personality traits

Modern theories of personality can still be traced back to the early work of Galton from 1869 onwards, who attempted to group the words we use to describe personality into a classification scheme. It was only after the Second World War that the scientific measurement of personality really came into being with the work of Cattell.

Cattell began by asking individuals to rate each other using the descriptions of personality used in everyday language. His review of the data suggested that there were no more than about 50 underlying dimensions. Further work with larger samples and the advanced statistical techniques led to his conclusions that there were no more than 12 Life (L) factors involved. Cattell then began to devise questionnaire items to measure these 12 factors and subsequently identified a further four factors (Q) from an analysis of the questionnaire returns.

The 16 primary factors identified by Cattell now contained in the 16PF test are as follows:

| | | | | | | |
|---|---|---|---|---|---|---|
| A | Warmth | F | Liveliness | L | Vigilance | Q1 Openness to |
| B | Reasoning | G | Rule- | M | Abstractness | change |
| C | Emotional | | consciousness | N | Privateness | Q2 Self-reliance |
| | stability | H | Social boldness | O | Apprehension | Q3 Perfectionism |
| E | Dominance | I | Sensitivity | | | Q4 Tension |

Each factor is measured on a spectrum expressed as word pairs, eg *warmth* is measured on a scale of *reserved–warm*. These are often referred to as *bi-polar scales*, meaning that any individual will be placed somewhere on the continuum between two extremes. What is important about this approach is that there is no right or wrong personality and the only issue that is important is how typical or unusual you are in relation to the rest of the population.

## Jungian typology

Psychological type is a theory developed by Carl Jung (1875–1961) to explain some of the apparently random differences in people's behaviour. Following extensive work on clients and others, Jung discovered predictable and differing patterns of behaviour. His theory of personality type recognised the existence of distinct patterns and provided an explanation for how these types develop.

According to Jung, differences in behaviour are caused by differences in the way people like to use their minds. The central idea is that when your mind is active, you are involved in one of two key mental activities:

1  taking information in, ie *perceiving*; or
2  organising that information internally and coming to conclusions, ie *judging*.

In turn, Jung observed that there were two opposite ways of *Perceiving*, which he called *Sensing* and *Intuition* and two opposite ways of *Judging*, which he called *Thinking* and *Feeling*. Everyone uses these essential processes on a daily basis, both towards the external world of people, things and events (*Extraversion*) and towards the inner world of ideas, thought and reflection (*Introversion*).

Jung believed that everyone has a natural preference for

using one kind of Perceiving and one kind of Judging, and he observed that each was drawn towards either the external or internal world. This idea was later expanded by Katherine Cook Briggs and her daughter, Isabel Briggs Myers and used to develop the Myers–Briggs Type Indicator (MBTI®) instrument.

Today, the Myers–Briggs Type Inventory (MBTI®) is one of the most widely used personality tests and has been translated into a number of languages. It can provide considerable insight into the way an individual relates to others, his/her preferred team role and work environment.

The MBTI® is based on Jung's typology and reports your preference on four scales, each consisting of two opposite poles:

- **Extraversion or Introversion (E–I)** – where you prefer to focus your attention on.
- **Sensing** or **Intuition (S–N)** – the way you prefer to take in information.
- **Thinking** or **Feeling (T–F)** – the way you prefer to make decisions.
- **Judging** or **Perceiving (J–P)** – the way you orientate yourself to the outside world.

Combinations of these four scales give us 16 different types as shown below. Each type can be referred to by a four-letter code.

So an **ISTJ** is a person who:

**I** – draws energy from and pays attention to their inner world,

| | ST<br>Sensing-<br>Thinking | SF<br>Sensing-<br>Feeling | NF<br>Intuitive-<br>Feeling | NT<br>Intuitive-<br>Thinking |
|---|---|---|---|---|
| IJ Introvert-Judging | ISTJ | ISFJ | INFJ | INTJ |
| IP Introvert-Perceiving | ISTP | ISFP | INFP | INTP |
| EP Extravert-Perceiving | ESTP | ESFP | ENFP | ENTP |
| EJ Extravert-Judging | ESTJ | ESFJ | ENFJ | ENTJ |

S – likes to take in information through the senses,
T – prefers to rely on logic rather than feelings when
    making decisions, and
J – likes to regulate and control life.

Their opposite number with different preferences on all
four scales would be an ENFP who:

E – draws energy from the outer world of people and
    events,
N – likes to take in information by looking at the big picture
    and making their own connections between facts,
F – relies a lot on feelings to make decisions, and
P – uses their perception a lot in reacting to the world.

Many managers fall into the **ESTJ** type. Here is an
abbreviated description of the type:

*'Practical, realistic and matter-of-fact with a natural ability for*
*practical subjects like business or mechanics. They are not*
*interested in abstract theories and expect their learning to have*
*immediate and practical application. They love to organise and*

> run activities. *They are decisive, acting quickly to implement decisions and can be relied upon to pay attention to practical, routine issues.'*

This seems to be a pretty good description of a typical manager. Of course this does not mean that the other types make poor managers and a quick review of the others will highlight those types who make great leaders (eg ENTJ) or entrepreneurs (eg INTJ).

Typologies have one great advantage – they are easy to understand and to relate to. They are often a great tool for developing individuals and for increasing their awareness of some of their main patterns of behaviour and how others see them. This approach also stresses a key principle about the use of personality scales – there is no right or wrong preference. On the other hand, typologies are generally less suited to selection, because they are too simplistic and do not allow us to discriminate clearly between individuals.

## The 'Big Five'

Sooner or later if you talk to anyone about personality tests, you will hear them mention the Big Five. These arose from the work of Costa and McCrae in 1985, who studied the results of a range of personality questionnaires using factor analysis and who identified 5 *big factors* that could explain most of the personality space covered by all these different measures. On the basis of this research they designed the NEO-Personality Inventory which measures differences between individuals on these five dimensions as described below.

1   Neuroticism
**High scorers** are generally more sensitive, emotional and prone to feelings that are upsetting, such as guilt or sadness. **Low scorers** are emotionally secure, resistant and relaxed individuals even under very stressful conditions.

2   Extraversion
**High scorers** are extraverted, outgoing, active and high-spirited. They prefer to be around people most of the time. **Low scorers** are introverted, reserved and serious. They prefer to be alone or with a few close friends.

3   Openness to experience
**High scorers** are open to new experiences with broad interests and a strong imagination. **Low scorers** are down-to-earth, practical, traditional and pretty much set in their ways.

4   Agreeableness
**High scorers** are compassionate, good-natured and generally eager to cooperate and avoid conflict. **Low scorers** are hard-headed, sceptical, proud and competitive. They tend to express their anger directly and forcefully.

5   Conscientiousness
**High scorers** are conscientious and well organised. They have high standards and always strive to achieve their goals. **Low scorers** are easy-going, not very well organised and sometimes rather careless. They prefer not to make plans if they can help it.

In fact, these five factors can be related to the global factors found in multi-factor tests like the 16PFV5 and 15FQ. They also link to the dimensions in the Jungian typology.

Sometimes the computer printouts from personality tests provide values for dimensions contained in other tests such as the Belbin Roles Inventory, Leadership and Subordinate Styles and Jungian types. These are estimates provided by the test designers and should be treated with caution.

Since the publication of Costa and McCrae's work the issue of the Big Five has attracted a lot of controversy, mainly on the grounds that they cannot cover all aspects of personality. However, a number of studies across a wide range of occupational groups have, in fact, shown correlations between ratings on these dimensions and job performance criteria.

## Behavioural roles in teambuilding

Questionnaires like the Myers–Briggs Type Indicator and Belbin's Team Role Inventory can provide considerable insight into the way a person interrelates with others, their preferred role in group situations and their favoured work environment. This can prove enormously useful for managers constructing their teams from scratch, but can also help members of an established team understand each other's strengths and weaknesses and avoid dangerous blind spots in the way a team functions. Where there is a strong organisational culture, it is common for teams to be composed of very similar types, with a significant absence of some key roles.

The Belbin Team Role Inventory is widespread in its use and recognition. In many organisations, the development that goes with certain levels of seniority is often accompanied by some consideration of the team roles. For this reason, and because of its high face validity, it is worth considering briefly the Inventory itself.

Dr Meredith Belbin, in his research on behaviour with people in group environments, suggested that there are eight primary roles that people adopt in teams.

The eight roles are:

### 1  Shaper
Sets the agenda; is the driver of the objectives and priorities.
*Dominant and dynamic.*

### 2  Chairman
Controls the way in which the team moves towards the group objectives; makes the team cohere.
*Dominant and dynamic.*

### 3  Monitor–Evaluator
Analyses problems and evaluates ideas and suggestions.
*Analytical, tenacious – a critic.*

### 4  Plant
Generates ideas and new approaches.
*Unorthodox, intelligent and imaginative.*

### 5  Team Worker
Supports team members, builds team spirit.
*Diplomatic and sympathetic.*

### 6  Company Worker
Translates into action.
*Stable, cautious, organised.*

### 7  Completer Finisher
Oriented on achievement of goals and completion of tasks.

*Disciplined and conscientious.*

### 8  *Resource–Investigator*
Communicates with the outside world.
*Extravert, enthusiastic and likeable*

There is a simple self-scored test that will help you to define your own preferred team role, and team role profile. It has proved very useful when members of a team share and discuss their own preferred team roles and how this operates in terms of the actual team processes.

## The limitations of personality questionnaires

Personality and personal values questionnaires are relatively cheap and easy to administer and score, but are certainly less reliable and valid than tests of mental ability. Little or no evidence of criterion validity (ie relevance to the job) has been found for many personality tests and scales. The fact that the questions themselves often have no direct relevance to the workplace does not help. In some well-documented cases, their value in selecting people from unusual backgrounds or different cultures has been questioned because test design is heavily influenced by culture.

This does not mean, however, that personality tests do not have an important role to play in organisations. But they must be used intelligently and test users must be aware of their limitations. Even a perfect test (if it existed!) can be misused and most of the examples used to criticise the use of personality tests are due to misuse of the test rather than test design. The two most important stages of test use – **interpretation** and **using the results to make decisions** – are profoundly influenced by the situation they are being

used for and may be left in the hands of those with
insufficient expertise.

## Misinterpretation of tests

Personality tests are very open to misinterpretation. Your
stated preference is just that – it does not mean you always
behave that way and it does need to be placed in the
context of your experience, acquired skills and
environment. For example, if you are a strong introvert,
this does not mean that you are automatically shy, retiring
and unable to perform well in social situations. In reality
we all acquire skills that enable us to perform well in areas
that may not be our natural preference. There are many
managers and public speakers who are viewed as extreme
extraverts but who are actually the opposite – their
lifestyle and job has taught them to behave as extraverts.

Inappropriate use of personality tests sometimes leads
organisations to arrive at the wrong conclusions and to take
bad decisions. In selection, for example, you can only use
the results of tests successfully if you have shown key
features of personality to be critical to the job and to have
correctly interpreted the results for individuals. This is why
the use of tests is usually strictly controlled. To get the best
out of the results, they need to be interpreted by qualified
staff and the interpretation confirmed after discussing
issues with the test-taker. Ultimately, the test-taker is
probably the best judge of the accuracy of the report, which
is why detailed feedback is usually advised.

## Does your personality profile change?

Generally the profiles of most individuals remain stable at
least over several years. However, they can be affected by

periods of change or stress and this does need to be taken into account when you receive feedback. Over longer periods of time there is no doubt that individuals may 'drift' on individual scales, usually because they have learned new skills and ways of thinking. People working in highly disciplined professions like the law or science may develop profiles matching the job requirements more closely. There seems to be some evidence that some effective managers can develop more balanced profiles as they increase their repertoire of behavioural skills (notably in Introversion–Extraversion).

# Summary

- Personality tests are generally based on two main approaches to personality – personality trait and personality type or typologies.
- Tests based on trait theory (eg the 16PF questionnaire) place individuals somewhere on a scale between two extremes for a number of factors or dimensions.
- Tests based on personality types (eg the MBTI questionnaire) allocate individuals to particular types. Typologies are easy to understand and useful for development purposes.
- Personality questionnaires need to be interpreted carefully, because there is a clear difference between stated preferenes and actual behaviour.

In the next chapter, we shall provide details of some of the main personality questionnaires available commercially.

# The main types of personality test

In this chapter, we shall provide a brief résumé of a range of tests commonly used in employment practice. For each of these tests, information is provided under the following headings:

- General details
- Uses
- Format
- What does it measure?

## 16PF Questionnaire

*General details*

One of the most popular questionnaires, first introduced in 1949. It was the original 16-factor test developed by Cattell that has spawned many similar 15–17-factor tests. Recently updated, first as version 5 (16PF5) and most recently as an industrial version.

*Uses*

Used by personnel professionals for selection, development and even clinical purposes in many countries. In the UK, it is most often used for selecting graduates, sales, managerial, professional and technical staff.

*Format*

Available as a booklet or computer form. There are 185 questions, to be answered as True, False or Not sure. It takes about 35 minutes to answer.

*What does it measure?*

As the name implies it measures 16 primary factors (PF) as follows:

| | |
|---|---|
| • Warmth | • Vigilance |
| • Reasoning | • Abstractedness |
| • Emotional stability | • Privateness |
| • Dominance | • Apprehension |
| • Liveliness | • Openness to change |
| • Rule-consciousness | • Self-reliance |
| • Social boldness | • Perfectionism |
| • Sensitivity | • Tension |

In turn, these are combined to provide values on five global factors, that are equivalent to the Big Five:

- Extraversion
- Anxiety
- Tough-mindedness
- Independence
- Self-control

## 15FQ

*General details*

A similar instrument to the 16PF produced by Psytech International. There are a number of questionnaires similar to the 16PF in existence, but all are based on 15–17 primary factors and a number of global factors.

*Uses*
The same as the 16PF.

*Format*
The test is available in the questionnaire version and as a computerised test that can be administered at a distance. It generally takes about half an hour to complete, slightly less than the 16PF, due to the absence of reasoning questions.

*What does it measure?*
As the name implies the test measures 15 scales (it does not include the general intelligence items) and 5 global factors. Although these scales are similar, there are some subtle differences between them.

# Belbin Team Roles

*General details*
Popular due to availability of the questionnaire in the public domain, the Belbin Team Role Inventory test has its fans and critics. It does allow companies to combine personal development, teambuilding activities and job analysis within one activity.

*Uses*
The questionnaire is widely used in organisations to develop teams.

*Format*
The full package contains three components – a self report, a peer report and a job profiling form. The self report (which is often found in colleges and schools in its older version) and the job profiling report require the respondent to allocate a score of ten to descriptions of each of the team

roles. The peer report asks respondents to identify adjectives that best describe and least describe the person they are evaluating.

*What does it measure?*
The questionnaire provides a profile of an individual's preferred team roles as discussed in Chapter 2, which can be used to develop teamworking skills, but also to match individuals to specific jobs and roles.

# Myers–Briggs Type Indicator (MBTI®)

*General details*
The MBTI is one of the most widely used tests in the world today. It is supported by an impressive framework of materials to support its interpretation and application.

*Uses*
The questionnaire has an extremely wide following and is used in personal, career and marital counselling, executive development programmes, education and as a primary research tool. Many personality questionnaires are validated using the MBTI as a reference point because of its established position.

*Format*
It is available in two forms as a 126-item (Form G) or 166-item (Form F) questionnaire, either as a paper-pencil test or computerised questionnaire. It takes about 20–30 minutes to complete.

*What does it measure?*
As discussed in the last chapter, the MBTI identifies the Jungian type for an individual. It can be a powerful tool to help individuals recognise the impact of their personality on behaviour.

## NEO Five-Factor Inventory (NEO-FFI) and Personality Inventory (NEO-PI)

*General details*

These two questionnaires are based on the work of Costa and McRae and evaluate you against the Big Five factors. Easy to administer and score, this questionnaire is useful for group work.

*Uses*

Used in clinical psychology, counselling, career development and industrial psychology.

*Format*

NEO-FFI is a 60-item multiple-choice questionnaire and is a shortened version of the Personality Inventory (NEO-PI). NEO-PI is an 181-item test and is available in two forms; Form S for self-administration and Form R for observer ratings. These two questionnaires are available in computerised versions.

*What does it measure?*

The five domains are Neuroticism (N), Extraversion (E), Openness to Experience (O), Agreeableness (A) and Conscientiousness (C), as discussed earlier in Chapter 2. Separate scales for NEO-PI provide a more detailed analysis of personality:

- **Neuroticism (N)** – Anxiety, Hostility, Depression, Self-Consciousness, Impulsiveness and Vulnerability.
- **Extraversion (E)** – Warmth, Gregariousness, Assertiveness, Activity, Excitement-seeking and Positive Emotions.
- **Openness to Experience (O)** – Fantasy, Aesthetics, Feelings, Actions, Ideas and Values.

# OPQ

*General details*

The Occupational Personality Questionnaire is one of the best-known instruments and is offered by Saville & Holdsworth. First introduced in 1984, it is now available in a number of different formats and language versions.

*Uses*

OPQ occupies a key position in the market, being used by many selection and recruitment agencies and top companies. It is one of the few questionnaires that specifically set out to measure personality dimensions related to work performance. It is available in nine different versions and in various languages.

*Format*

The questionnaires can either be administered using the traditional question booklets and separate answer sheets or by using a computer. There are two main formats – one consists of 100 sets of four statements that require you to indicate which is most and which is least like you, for example:

I am a person who ...

- enjoys taking risks
- likes talking to people
- often feels upset
- is competitive.

The alternative format has 248 statements, each one of which is rated on a scale of 1 (Strongly Disagree) to 5 (Strongly Agree), for example:

- I like talking to strangers.
- I always do what I say I will do.
- I cope well with stress.

Depending on the version used, the test can take anything between ten minutes and one hour to complete.

*What does it measure?*

The longest version of the questionnaire measures 30 personality scales:

| | | |
|---|---|---|
| • Persuasive | • Detail-conscious | • Traditional |
| • Controlling | • Conscientious | • Change-orientated |
| • Independent | • Relaxed | • Conceptual |
| • Outgoing | • Worrying | • Emotional control |
| • Affiliative | • Tough-minded | • Optimistic |
| • Socially confident | • Caring | • Critical |
| • Modest | • Practical | • Active |
| • Democratic | • Data rational | • Competitive |
| • Innovative | Artistic | Achieving |
| • Forward-planning | • Behavioural | • Decisive |

The shortest version only measures six scales as follows:

- Imaginative
- Methodical
- Achieving
- Gregarious
- Emotional
- Sympathetic

# California Personality Inventory (CPI)

*General details*

This general-purpose personality questionnaire has been a firm favourite since its launch in the 1950s. Originally developed for use in the USA, it has since been updated and is available in two forms with 309 (CPI 309) and 434 (CPI 434) questions respectively.

*Uses*

It is widely used by organisations for the selection of managers and other staff. Often used for testing leadership and creativity, it can also be used for counselling and career development purposes.

*Format*

The questionnaire comes as a booklet and separate answer sheet, each question requiring you to answer true or false.

The questionnaire takes about 30 minutes to answer in the shorter version and 50 minutes in the longer version.

*What does it measure?*

The shorter version measures 14 personality scales as follows:

|  |  |
|---|---|
| • Dominance | • Achievement through conformance |
| • Social presence | • Achievement through independence |
| • Empathy | • Flexibility |
| • Socialisation | • Creativity |
| • Self-control | • Outgoingness |
| • Good impression | • Organisation |
| • Tolerance | • Self-realisation |

The longer version provides values for an additional nine scales:

- Status
- Sociability
- Self-acceptance
- Independence responses
- Responsibility
- Well-being
- Intellectual efficiency
- Tough-mindedness
- Communality or unusual

## Alternative forms of personality test

The purpose of this book is not to provide a complete digest of all of the tests, or indeed, of all of the test types that are available. We would need much more space to do that. However, there are many other tests and classes of test that we have barely covered, and we shall use this section to paint a picture of just some of those that are available.

One class of tests that are used for research, clinical and therapeutic purposes have little relevance to organisational life and we will not consider them here. The famous Rorschach inkblot test, in which subjects are asked to say what they can see in a series of inkblot is just one example.

However, there is another group of tests that we have not yet discussed, and these relate to values and interests. In fact, there are many such tests that give information about what people value, their life and career interests. An example is the work of Holland who classified career theme interests into the following categories:

- Realistic
- Investigative
- Artistic
- Social
- Enterprising
- Conventional.

Here are some other aspects of personal and behavioural preference for which there are test instruments:

- Selling or negotiation styles
- Management style
- Conflict style
- Creativity
- Motivation
- Stress
- Leadership
- Honesty and integrity
- And many more.

## Alternative ways of assessing personality

It may seem a strange comment, but the fact that personality questionnaires are cheap and easy to administer is one of their greatest weaknesses. For many organisations, it is too easy just to pick out a questionnaire for use in the selection process and to send the responses to a bureau for computer printouts. A test is only as good as the care that has gone into its selection and interpretation.

In fact, there are many other ways of assessing the personality of applicants, including the following:

- **Selection interviews**: this is the traditional way of making judgements on personality, but as we have already seen it is usually flawed. Properly structured interview questions can be used to confirm the results of personality questionnaires.
- **Handwriting analysis**: in some cultures and some organisations, handwriting is used to analyse various aspects of personality. However, no evidence for its effectiveness in selecting people has been found to date.
- **Social settings**: sometimes candidates are placed deliberately in a social setting (eg dinner) or a group situation (eg a problem-solving exercise) to observe their behaviour. Usually trained observers are used to provide observations on a candidate's sociability and behaviour.
- **Situational interviews**: walking a candidate through various scenarios that commonly occur in the workplace or asking them to talk about the qualities associated with success can provide a valuable insight into their personal values and attitudes. It is obvious that such interviews need to be carefully designed and carried out by trained interviewers.
- **Assessment centres**: commonly used by larger companies for selection, the assessment centre is simply a collection of different exercises to assess candidates against a range of criteria. All of the techniques described above may be used. Typically assessment centres last one or two days and are followed by a detailed feedback session.

# Summary

- We have looked at the range of types of test available under the headings of General details, Uses, Format and What does it measure?
- Most personality questionnaires have a similar format.
- There are many questionnaires that evaluate specific qualities related to the workplace (eg selling style).
- Personality questionnaires are just one tool in the list of techniques available for assessing personality.

In the next chapter, we shall examine the test experience itself more closely to ensure you get the most out of the experience.

# Preparing yourself for personality tests

In the last chapter, we examined some of the key
personality tests to give you an insight into their format and
their main uses. In this chapter, we will examine the test
experience itself to prepare you for the event.

There is no doubt that sitting tests can be stressful for many
people. The reasons can be varied – fear of the unknown, a
hate of formal 'test' situations left over from school days,
personal insecurity – but whatever the cause, if you do feel
nervous just remember that this is a perfectly natural
reaction. More to the point, you can deal with your anxiety
by being prepared. We shall deal with this possibility by
explaining the procedures for test administration, the
simple steps you can take to prepare yourself, your rights as
a test-taker and finally what you can do to maximise the
experience.

## Test administration

Personality tests are generally used as part of the selection
process for jobs or as part of an internal development
process. In either case, it is common for employers to use a
battery of tests (ie more than one). Usually this involves
several aptitude tests followed by a personality
questionnaire.

The process you will go through when asked to take a
personality test is pretty standard, because organisations
need to take special care to make sure everyone goes
through the same experience. This is why 'to some' the
whole experience can be rather formal and off-putting, just

like an examination. This is probably what you will experience.

1 A qualified test administrator will introduce you to the test. They will usually explain the reason for the test, even if you have been provided with the information previously.
2 They will then check that you have everything you need for the test, such as the test itself, an answer sheet or book, pencils and/or pens, erasers, paper for scribbling on.
3 You will then be asked to record your name and date on the answer sheet, perhaps with some biographical details.
4 The administrator will then read out the instructions at the beginning of the questionnaire. Follow these carefully, even if you think they look simple. These typically include (a) how to record your answers and change them, (b) the fact that there are no 'correct' answers and the need to answer these as truthfully as you can and (c) some advice to avoid middle responses and not to spend too long on questions. Once they have read through the instructions, they will ask if you have any questions.
5 You will then be asked to begin. During the test, the administrator will walk round the room to check that you are completing the answer sheet correctly. They are not checking to see if you are 'cheating'.
6 When the test has been completed, the administrator will take in all the materials, thank you for sitting the test and perhaps remind you what is going to happen to it.

All this is pretty simple. One key difference between aptitude or ability tests and personality questionnaires is that the former are timed, whereas personality questionnaires are open, so you can take as long as you like. A short questionnaire can take as little as ten minutes, whereas the longer ones can take up to 45 minutes.

## Preparing for tests

So, you have been short-listed for that important job and asked to take a personality test. You may feel a little nervous. Remember, this is perfectly normal and easily treated. There is a lot you can do to prepare for the test itself, for example:

- research the job properly
- find out more about yourself
- relax and be yourself.

*Researching the job properly*
Organisations don't use personality questionnaires just for the sake of it. They use these tests because certain personal qualities have been linked directly to job success. If they have done their work thoroughly, a lot of time will have been spent analysing the job in question to arrive at a person specification, which in turn has then been linked to the tests being used. Of course, this isn't always the case, but job adverts and descriptions still reveal a lot about the qualities being sought and the organisation itself. Here is one short piece from an advert in *The Times*.

*The successful candidate will be energetic with a naturally sunny disposition. The abilities to manage a busy workload, to think ahead and to work under pressure are vital. A committed, precise and organised approach is essential.*

In a short paragraph, the company has revealed quite a lot about the match between the person they are looking for and the job. These are not just words – they can give you vital information about your suitability and the desirability of the job. In the table on page 52 the key words have been cross-referenced to some of the key personality descriptions in the 16PF questionnaire.

*Finding out more about yourself*
If you examine the descriptions in this table, you may find yourself quickly identifying with one of the two boxes. You are beginning to profile yourself. As you go down the table, you will begin to get a sense of your match with the job. Of course you would need to find out more about the job and to confirm that the description is accurate. But the more you analyse any information the company has provided, the more insight you will gain into the job and whether it suits you. We all like good pay, conditions and a description that sounds exciting, but is it really you?

Spending some time on this task should help you to relax but, more to the point, it will focus your mind on asking the right questions at interview. Just how far do their expectations go, when they say they want someone energetic? Do they mean lively or the ability to endure a 20-hour day?

Finding out more about the measures used to assess

| Job description phrase | Key qualities being sought | The type of person the job would not suit |
|---|---|---|
| Energetic | High energy. Lively. Forceful. Assertive. | Relaxed. Patient. Serious. Restrained. Careful. Deferential. |
| Sunny disposition | Warm. Socially bold. Attentive to others. Group-orientated. | Shy. Reserved. Self-reliant. Individualistic. |
| Manages a busy workload | Lively. Likes to be kept busy. | Serious. Restrained. Careful. |
| Works well under pressure | Copes well with stress. Placid. Emotionally stable. | Temperamental. Self-doubting. |
| Committed | Can be trusted to get on with things. Conscious of the rules. Dutiful. Will fit in well with group decisions. | Non-conforming. Expedient, does what is necessary. |
| Precise | Loves to do things meticulously with attention to detail. Perfectionist. Self-disciplined. | Flexible. Tolerates uncertainty and disorder. Undemanding. |
| Organised | Likes their life to be in order. Probably very practical. | Flexible people who cope well with uncertainty and disorder. |

personality and even taking some of these tests will equip you with a much better understanding of yourself. It will also allow you to position yourself more accurately against the qualities being sought by different employers.

We will return to this issue in the next chapter to help you develop this skill further.

*Relaxing and being yourself*
Always remember with personality questionnaires that there are not really any right or wrong answers. Acting naturally and getting yourself into a fairly relaxed frame of mind is probably the best advice anyone can give to help you 'do well'.

Before the test, you should:

- Get a good night's rest and avoid anything that may upset your normal mental balance, such as pub crawls.
- Arrive with plenty of time to spare, but not so much that you have hours to worry about the test(s).
- If anxiety is getting the better of you, make a conscious effort to breathe slowly and deeply and to turn your attention to something else if possible.

During the test itself, here are some golden rules that you should follow:

- Avoid extremes – don't select options you think will impress or make you stand out.
- Be positive – some people can be too hard on themselves or are completely unrealistic. Think yourself into the frame of mind you experience at the end of a good day's work.

- Don't try to second-guess the questions – you are unlikely to have sufficient knowledge of the test's construction and would have to maintain your logic throughout the test.
- Don't pull the questions apart – if you find yourself thinking 'well, it depends' or 'I'm not sure I would really do either. I would go for another option', then please stop. Questionnaires are designed to  force you to choose between options. Listen to your first impression.
- Be as honest as you can – go with your gut reaction.

A well-designed test will have in-built measures to check that you are completing the questionnaire properly. If you try to distort your responses, this will almost certainly be identified and could have a damaging effect on your application. The advice given by the administrator at the beginning of the exercise – to answer as honestly as possible and avoid spending time deliberating over the questions really covers all of these points. It is almost impossible to keep track of all the questions involved and in trying to affect the results, you may be wrong in your assumptions about what the employer is looking for or may cover over some of your best qualities.

If you remain unconvinced by this argument, you should remember that you will need to live up to this artificial profile at the interview itself or, even worse, in the job itself.

## Know your rights

No organisation can force you to take tests. They are obliged to secure your agreement to take any test and because the results are of an extremely personal nature, they have a legal and ethical responsibility to make sure the results are used, interpreted, stored and disposed of safely.

You can, of course, refuse to complete tests, but in reality the organisation will be within its rights to reject your application. Nevertheless, you do have well-defined rights as a test-taker. Here are a few guidelines about the correct use of tests.

*Information*
Responsible organisations should take special steps to ensure there are no misunderstandings and that the test-takers fully understand the purpose of the tests. They have a duty to make sure you are fully informed about the nature of the tests, their role in the recruitment process and their likely duration, the arrangements for taking the tests and what will be done with the results. If in doubt, ask!

*Test administration*
The facilities used for the administration of any test are important. You have a right to be provided with a quiet, well-illuminated and ventilated room, complete with comfortable and well-spaced tables and chairs. The test itself must be carried out by a qualified administrator and free from any interruptions, otherwise the test itself is really invalidated.

*Equal opportunities*
The issue of the cultural or sexual sensitivity of tests is a difficult one. In law it is the responsibility of the organisation to check that the tests used are not discriminatory because they contain elements that are culturally biased (typically questions that ask you about your favourite activities). If you have any concerns, you do

have a right to check that the test has been screened for cultural bias by testing it among different groups.

However, in some situations, different cultural types may show personality differences that can be linked to job performance. Here, the organisation may be quite justified in using such tests, but would need to be very confident about their validity, measured in terms of job performance and success.

If in doubt, you could seek guidance from an expert in the field or from the Equal Opportunities Commission.

*Special needs*
If you have any special needs, discuss these with the organisation. You do not need to suffer in silence and you may be pleasantly surprised by the alternatives that are available. For example, computerised versions with large text for the visually impaired can make life a lot easier.

*Test feedback*
Ideally all test-takers should be given an opportunity to receive feedback and to discuss the results of the questionnaire. In reality, where these tests are used for selection, there may be too many candidates or the organisation may not wish to reveal too much about the selection criteria used.

Even if you do not receive formal feedback, you may receive it informally during the interview through any questions that ask you about your personal preferences and management style. Watch for these and remember this is where your preparation can really pay off.

Finally, all candidates should receive the same treatment.

This means that restricting detailed feedback to internal candidates because of the numbers involved is very bad selection practice indeed.

*Security and access*
Your test results are an extremely personal and sensitive form of information. For this reason, the organisation has a duty to ensure that access to the results is restricted only to those people who are qualified to interpret them and those who will actually use the results. In agreeing to take the test, you have only agreed to it being used in the situation that has been requested. The organisation is not at liberty to use the results elsewhere.

The test results should be kept in a secure location, under lock and key, and are (from October 1998) subject to the full protection of the Data Protection Act.

*Disposal of results*
Test results have a limited lifespan. They should not be kept any longer than the event they were required for. You are quite within your rights to ask how long the results will be kept and how they will be disposed of.

## Getting the most out of the experience

Whatever the outcome of a process involving the use of psychometric tests, you should take steps to maximise your learning. Even if you fail to get that brilliant job, you should follow up the interview by asking for feedback. Good organisations will normally be open to requests for more information than the simple acceptance or rejection letter. If you are given an opportunity to discuss your performance in detail, make sure you identify the critical factors involved.

- Ask about the relative importance of the personality questionnaire compared to experience and specific skills.
- Identify the key qualities they were looking for.
- Try to identify any qualities that worked against you during the process.
- Focus sharply on the issues involved with these critical factors. Don't just get annoyed – ask them directly what they were looking for and how this compared with their assessment of you.
- Listen to their advice on how to improve your profile.

Even if you don't receive this sort of feedback, try to be objective about your performance using the same framework. You may find it helpful to involve a trusted colleague or boss in this process. Above all, be determined to learn more about yourself from the experience and identify clear action points for the future. Even if you don't get the job, gaining more insight into your most marketable qualities and those which perhaps work against you in some situations will equip you better for the next application. Successful managers often have profiles that change over time. One secret to their success is almost certainly that they do pay attention to the way others see them, that they recognise barriers to progress and are able to adjust their work behaviour accordingly.

## Summary

In this chapter, we have examined three main factors involved in taking tests, and how to ensure you get the best out of them:

- How tests are administered
- How to prepare effectively for the tests
- Your rights as a test-taker
- After the test, how to get the most out of it.

In the next chapter, we shall provide you with a sample personality questionnaire to familiarise you with the type of questions you will typically encounter in these tests. It will also provide you with more insight into how tests are constructed. Perhaps more importantly, the results will link with the final chapter, in which we will show you how to gain more control over your personal preferences and their relationship to career preferences.

# Test yourself

In the last chapter, we reviewed the test experience itself to give you an idea of what to expect and to provide some insight into the way personality questionnaires are used. We stressed the fact that anxiety over taking 'tests' was quite natural, but something that everyone can deal with.

One of the best ways of dealing with the fear of the unknown is to take someone through the process to explain what is involved and therefore to de-mystify everything. This is what we propose to do in this chapter by taking you through an example questionnaire. This will help you understand how tests are designed and what they are actually measuring. The profile you develop in this chapter should also be useful for the last chapter.

## A Simple Five-Factor Questionnaire (SFFQ)

The following questionnaire has been designed to provide a rough guide to your personality preferences based on a five-factor model. It has, however, been deliberately simplified and the results should not be taken as a definitive evaluation of your personality. Please read the instructions carefully before embarking on the test.

*The instructions*
This is a questionnaire concerning your interests, preferences and attitudes about a range of things. There is no time limit, but most people take about ten minutes to complete the questionnaire. Please read all the instructions carefully before beginning.

Answer each question by filling in the box that best describes you, for example:

| Strongly agree | Agree | In-between | Disagree | Strongly disagree |
|---|---|---|---|---|
| SA | A | I | D | SD |

I like to read novels.    ☐     ☐ ☐     ☐     ☐

When answering questions, please remember the following:

- Use pencil to record your answers.
- Don't spend too much time deliberating over the questions. The information provided may not be as full as you would like, but please try to answer the questions as best as you can.
- Please avoid the middle (in between) answer wherever possible.
- Try to be as truthful as you can. Don't give an answer just because it seems to be the right thing to say.
- Make sure you answer every question, even those that you feel don't apply directly to you.
- If you want to change an answer, erase your original response and add your altered response.

Now begin.

**?** ## Test Yourself

| | | Strongly agree | Agree | In-between | Disagree | Strongly disagree |
|---|---|---|---|---|---|---|
| | | SA | A | I | D | SD |
| 1 | I am always happy to see my friends. | ☐ | ☑ | ☐ | ☐ | ☐ |
| 2 | I do not require the company of other people. | ☐ | ☐ | ☐ | ☑ | ☐ |
| 3 | In group situations, I prefer others to take the lead. | ☐ | ☐ | ☐ | ☑ | ☐ |
| 4 | I think people's feelings need to be considered when making decisions. | ☐ | ☑ | ☐ | ☐ | ☐ |
| 5 | In order to get things done, it is often necessary to cut corners. | ☐ | ☐ | ☐ | ☑ | ☐ |
| 6 | I have trouble coping under pressure. | ☐ | ☐ | ☐ | ☑ | ☐ |
| 7 | At parties, others tend to be the centre of attention. | ☐ | ☐ | ☑ | ☐ | ☐ |
| 8 | I like to consider all alternatives carefully when making an important decision. | ☑ | ☐ | ☐ | ☐ | ☐ |

9  I prefer coming up with new ideas than turning them into practical reality. ☐ ☐ ☐ ☑ ☐

10  I like to have a routine to follow. ☐ ☐ ☑ ☐ ☐

11  I tend to accept people at face value. ☐ ☑ ☐ ☐ ☐

12  I believe important decisions are best made in a group situation. ☐ ☐ ☐ ☑ ☐

13  I like to think I am direct and honest in my dealings with others. ☐ ☑ ☐ ☐ ☐

14  I tend to prefer 'tried-and-tested' solutions. ☐ ☐ ☐ ☑ ☐

15  I do not allow myself to be affected much by other people's expectations. ☐ ☑ ☐ ☐ ☐

16  I generally succeed in anything I do. ☐ ☑ ☐ ☐ ☐

17  I have never hurt anyone knowingly. ☐ ☐ ☐ ☑ ☐

18  I like to take time to get to know people. ☐ ☑ ☐ ☐ ☐

19  I tend to take the lead in group situations. ☐ ☐ ☑ ☐ ☐

20  I tend to base my decisions on concrete evidence. ☐ ☐ ☑ ☐ ☐

21  I like to have the freedom to do things the way I want. ☐ ☑ ☐ ☐ ☐

22  I find it easy to express my emotions. ☐ ☑ ☐ ☐ ☐

23  I generally make the first move when getting to know new people. ☐ ☐ ☑ ☐ ☐

24  Some people think I am unpredictable and impulsive. ☐ ☑ ☐ ☐ ☐

25  I often spend time just to think about things. ☐ ☐ ☐ ☑ ☐

26  I am generally critical of the established way of doing things. ☐ ☐ ☐ ☐ ☑

27  I find it difficult to relax and unwind after a hard day's work. ☐ ☐ ☐ ☐ ☑

28   It is important to have the freedom to make your own decisions.  ☐ ☑ ☐ ☐ ☐

29   I give a lot of thought to the impact of my words and actions on others.  ☐ ☐ ☑ ☐ ☐

30   Rules are there to be broken.  ☐ ☐ ☐ ☑ ☐

31   Status is far less important than actual performance at work.  ☐ ☑ ☐ ☐ ☐

32   I tend to be rather critical of other people.  ☐ ☑ ☐ ☐ ☐

33   I can't ever think of a situation where I have let someone down.  ☐ ☐ ☐ ☑ ☐

34   I need regular social contact in my work to keep me happy.  ☐ ☑ ☐ ☐ ☐

35   I am always concerned with the needs of others.  ☐ ☑ ☐ ☐ ☐

36   I dislike emotionally charged situations.  ☐ ☐ ☑ ☐ ☐

37   It is always

|  |  |  |  |  |  |  |
|---|---|---|---|---|---|---|
|  | important to stick by the rules. | ☐ | ☐ | ☑ | ☐ | ☐ |
| 38 | When something is important, I tend to worry about my success. | ☐ | ☐ | ☐ | ☑ | ☐ |
| 39 | I enjoy being the centre of attention. | ☐ | ☐ | ☑ | ☐ | ☐ |
| 40 | I find it easy to deal with unplanned circumstances. | ☐ | ☑ | ☐ | ☐ | ☐ |
| 41 | I like to think of myself as pragmatic. | ☐ | ☑ | ☐ | ☐ | ☐ |
| 42 | I dislike work that involves rigidly following a set of procedures and systems. | ☐ | ☐ | ☑ | ☐ | ☐ |
| 43 | I tend to leave things to the last minute. | ☐ | ☑ | ☐ | ☐ | ☐ |
| 44 | I prefer group activities to working on my own. | ☐ | ☐ | ☑ | ☐ | ☐ |
| 45 | I like to make a good impression on others. | ☐ | ☑ | ☐ | ☐ | ☐ |
| 46 | I enjoy finding new ways of doing things. | ☑ | ☐ | ☐ | ☐ | ☐ |
| 47 | I think I am a fairly |  |  |  |  |  |

conventional person at heart. ☐ ☑ ☐ ☐ ☐

48 I think you should keep your emotions under control. ☐ ☐ ☑ ☐ ☐

49 I have never told a 'white lie'. ☐ ☐ ☐ ☐ ☑

50 I generally find it easy to get to know new people quickly. ☐ ☑ ☐ ☐ ☐

51 I am sometimes accused of being insensitive to the feelings of others. ☐ ☑ ☐ ☐ ☐

52 I can be deeply moved by a piece of poetry. ☐ ☑ ☐ ☐ ☐

53 I dislike too much change. ☐ ☐ ☑ ☐ ☐

54 I like to get to know someone well before I agree to do things. ☐ ☐ ☐ ☑ ☐

55 I feel nervous when in an unfamiliar, social situation. ☐ ☑ ☐ ☐ ☐

56 Most people see me as a very dependable person. ☐ ☑ ☐ ☐ ☐

57   I enjoy solving practical problems. ☐ ☑ ☐ ☐ ☐

58   I like to think of myself as a perfectionist. ☐ ☐ ☑ ☐ ☐

59   I sometimes feel I have let people down. ☐ ☑ ☐ ☐ ☐

60   It is important to have the support of your fellow workers. ☐ ☐ ☑ ☐ ☐

61   It is important to use tact and diplomacy to avoid hurting the feelings of others. ☐ ☑ ☐ ☐ ☐

62   Change is necessary to avoid stagnation. ☐ ☑ ☐ ☐ ☐

63   Self-control over your emotions is important. ☐ ☐ ☐ ☑ ☐

64   I find that tension makes me perform better. ☐ ☐ ☑ ☐ ☐

65   I have never worried about any of my mistakes. ☐ ☐ ☐ ☐ ☑

# Scoring the results

Transfer your results to the sections below and add up the scores, entering the total in the box labelled RAW SCORE at the bottom of the column.

*Extravert*

| Question number | SA | A | I | D | SD |
|---|---|---|---|---|---|
| 2 | 0 | 1 | 2 | (3) | 4 |
| 7 | 0 | 1 | (2) | 3 | 4 |
| 12 | 4 | 3 | 2 | (1) | 0 |
| 18 | 0 | (1) | 2 | 3 | 4 |
| 23 | 4 | 3 | (2) | 1 | 0 |
| 28 | 0 | (1) | 2 | 3 | 4 |
| 34 | 4 | (3) | 2 | 1 | 0 |
| 39 | 4 | 3 | (2) | 1 | 0 |
| 44 | 4 | (3) | 2 | 1 | 0 |
| 50 | 4 | (3) | 2 | 1 | 0 |
| 55 | 0 | (1) | 2 | 3 | 4 |
| 60 | 4 | 3 | (2) | 1 | 0 |
| RAW SCORE | | 12 | 8 | 4 | |

| | | | | | |
|---|---|---|---|---|---|
| | 1 | 3 | 2 | 2 | 1 |

## *Independent*

| Question number | SA | A | I | D | SD |
|---|---|---|---|---|---|
| 3 | 0 | 1 | 2 | (3) | 4 |
| 8 | (0) | 1 | 2 | 3 | 4 |
| 13 | 4 | (3) | 2 | 1 | 0 |
| 19 | 4 | 3 | (2) | 1 | 0 |
| 24 | 4 | (3) | 2 | 1 | 0 |
| 29 | 0 | 1 | (2) | 3 | 4 |
| 35 | 0 | (1) | 2 | 3 | 4 |
| 40 | 4 | (3) | 2 | 1 | 0 |
| 45 | 0 | (1) | 2 | 3 | 4 |
| 51 | 4 | (3) | 2 | 1 | 0 |
| 56 | 0 | (1) | 2 | 3 | 4 |
| 61 | 0 | (1) | 2 | 3 | 4 |
| RAW SCORE | 16 | 4 | 3 | | |
| | 1 | 4 | 2 | 2 | 1 |

## *Tough-minded*

| Question number | SA | A | I | D | SD |
|---|---|---|---|---|---|
| 4 | 0 | (1) | 2 | 3 | 4 |
| 9 | 0 | 1 | 2 | (3) | 4 |
| 14 | 4 | 3 | 2 | (1) | 0 |
| 20 | 4 | 3 | (2) | 1 | 0 |
| 25 | 0 | (1) | 2 | 3 | 4 |
| 30 | 0 | 1 | 2 | (3) | 4 |
| 36 | 4 | 3 | (2) | 1 | 0 |
| 41 | 4 | (3) | 2 | 1 | 0 |
| 46 | (0) | 1 | 2 | 3 | 4 |
| 52 | 0 | (1) | 2 | 3 | 4 |
| 57 | 4 | (3) | 2 | 1 | 0 |
| 62 | 0 | (1) | 2 | 3 | 4 |
| RAW SCORE | 10 | 4 | 7 | | |
| | 1 | 3 | 2 | 2 | 1 |

## *Conforming*

| Question number | SA | A | I | D | SD |
|---|---|---|---|---|---|
| 5 | 0 | (1) | 2 | 3 | 4 |
| 10 | 4 | 3 | (2) | 1 | 0 |
| 15 | 4 | 3 | 2 | (1) | 0 |
| 21 | 0 | (1) | 2 | 3 | 4 |
| 26 | 0 | 1 | 2 | 3 | (4) |
| 31 | 0 | (1) | 2 | 3 | 4 |
| 37 | 4 | 3 | (2) | 1 | 0 |
| 42 | 0 | 1 | (2) | 3 | 4 |
| 47 | 4 | (3) | 2 | 1 | 0 |
| 53 | 4 | 3 | (2) | 1 | 0 |
| 58 | 4 | 3 | (2) | 1 | 0 |
| 63 | 4 | 3 | 2 | (1) | 0 |
| RAW SCORE | 6 | 10 | 2 | 4 | |
| | 1 | 2 | 3 | 1 | 2 |

*Anxious*

| Question number | SA | A | I | D | SD |
|---|---|---|---|---|---|
| 6 | 4 | 3 | 2 | (1) | 0 |
| 11 | 0 | (1) | 2 | 3 | 4 |
| 16 | 0 | (1) | 2 | 3 | 4 |
| 22 | 4 | (3) | 2 | 1 | 0 |
| 27 | 4 | 3 | 2 | 1 | (0) |
| 32 | 4 | (3) | 2 | 1 | 0 |
| 38 | 4 | 3 | 2 | (1) | 0 |
| 43 | 4 | (3) | 2 | 1 | 0 |
| 48 | 0 | 1 | (2) | 3 | 4 |
| 54 | 4 | 3 | 2 | (1) | 0 |
| 59 | 4 | (3) | 2 | 1 | 0 |
| 64 | 4 | 3 | (2) | 1 | 0 |
| RAW SCORE | 14 | 4 | 3 | | |
| | 1 | 3 | 2 | 2 | 1 |

*Social Desirability*

| Question number | SA | A | I | D | SD |
|---|---|---|---|---|---|
| 1 | 4 | (3) | 2 | 1 | 0 |
| 17 | 4 | 3 | 2 | (1) | 0 |
| 33 | 4 | 3 | 2 | (1) | 0 |
| 49 | 4 | 3 | 2 | 1 | (0) |
| 65 | 4 | 3 | 2 | 1 | (0) |
| RAW SCORE | | 3 | | 2 | |

Now convert each of the raw scores into profile scores using the conversion table below, with the exception of the Social Desirability raw score.

| Converted score | Raw score |
|---|---|
| 1 | 0–3 |
| 2 | 4–9 |
| 3 | 10–15 |
| 4 | 16–21 |
| 5 | 22–27 |
| 6 | 28–33 |
| 7 | 34–39 |
| 8 | 40–45 |
| 9 | 46–48 |

Note your converted scores on the chart below:

| | 1 2 3 4 5 6 7 8 9 | | |
|---|---|---|---|
| Introversion | 2 2 1 | | Extraversion |
| Group-orientated | 2 2 1 | | Independent |
| Sentimental | 2 2 1 | | Tough-minded |
| Open | 2 2 1 | | Conforming |
| Confident | 2 2 1 | | Anxious |

You will see that your scores place you to the left or the right or the centre of the five scales. For instance, on the first scale, a 1 would be Introvert and a 9 Extrovert, with shades in between. You should not attach too much importance to these specific scores, however. Instead, you will find it more useful if you classify the results as follows:

| Converted score | Classification |
|---|---|
| 1 | Low scorer |
| 2–3 | Tendency towards low-scoring side of the scale (eg Introversion) |
| 4–6 | Balanced profile, average |
| 7–8 | Tendency towards high-scoring side of the scale (eg Extraversion) |
| 9 | High scorer |

Finally add up the total number of questions where you have ticked the In-between box (ie undecided) and enter in the box below:

Central responses

# Interpreting the results

Before we examine your profile, let's examine your questionnaire response trends. Many questionnaires use a variety of techniques to assess how honest your responses are. Here we have used two devices:

*Central tendency*
This measures how undecided you were when you completed the questionnaire. If you answered In-between to more than a third of the questions, it places a doubt on the validity of the results. You may genuinely have found it very difficult to choose, but in a real-life situation the test user would need to find out why this was the case.

*Social desirability*
If your score is greater than 10, then you need to ask yourself how honest you were in completing the questionnaire. For example, it is highly unlikely that you have never told a lie, although in some rare cases it is possible. Usually people achieve higher scores with these items because they want to be seen in a favourable light. Obviously in a real-life situation, the test user would want to be sure that the questionnaire results are accurate.

Now let's examine your profile for the five factors that you have entered into the table above. We are going to review these under three main headings:

1  Your interpersonal style – how you relate to others, involving two factors, *Extraversion* and *Independence*.

2   Your thinking style, involving two factors, *Tough-mindedness* and *Control*.

3   Your emotional style, expressed as *Confidence*.

Note: it is important to stress that the results do not have the same meaning as other, established tests, nor have they been standardised against national norms.

## Interpersonal style

The first two factors, Extraversion and Independence measure your preferences in dealing with other people.

*Factor 1: Introversion – Extraversion*
Extraversion is perhaps the most significant personality factor of all. It appears as the key characteristic in virtually all personality questionnaires and is generally listed as the first of the 'Big Five' factors of personality. Perhaps more than any other personality factor, extraversion is the most visible aspect of observed behaviour.

**High scorers (Extraverts)** have a strong inclination towards people. They are usually happiest in situations where they are surrounded by others and are able to engage in social interaction. They will be socially confident, uninhibited and will generally enjoy initiating and developing personal relationships. On the other hand, because they may be impulsive, they may not always think through the consequences of their actions. This tendency to rush in can often be seen as irresponsible and overpowering or rude.

At work, extraverts definitely prefer to work in teams or groups and do not like working on their own. They will prefer to seek out the views of others and to collaborate on projects. Extreme extraverts can be viewed as outspoken, often actively putting their views across rather assertively. This has obvious advantages where persuasive skills are required, such as in sales, marketing and tough negotiations.

**Low scorers (Introverts)** are generally quiet and reserved. They like to keep to themselves and are quite happy with their own thoughts and feelings. They do not actively need the company of others, will tend to feel uncomfortable in social situations and are unlikely to actively pursue social gatherings. They will not feel driven to exchange views with others and often are happiest engaged in solitary activities that do not involve constantly having to interact with people.

In the workplace, introverts are often seen as shy, rather restrained and somewhat distant or aloof. Consequently, they are often overlooked. They are usually good at working on their own or in small groups without needing to rely on outside support and guidance. This is an important asset in many jobs. Where they have good knowledge and expertise, introverts can be just as assertive as extraverts.

*Factor 2: Independence*
Independence reflects the desire to get things done and make things happen.

**The high scorer (Independent)** is seen as alert, quick to respond to situations, challenging, decisive in their decision-making, uncompromising and self-assured. They are agents of action, movement and change. They readily confront the status quo. Rarely taking no for an answer, high scorers may be a 'law unto themselves', their behaviour determined more by their own values and principles than the expectations of others.

**Low scorers (Group-orientated)** are much more people-orientated, empathic and sensitive, being more concerned with the needs of others than the need to accomplish a task expeditiously. Deliberating, cautious, passive and accommodating, their reactions to situations will often be influenced by concerns about the most acceptable behaviour in the eyes of others. Finding it easy to empathise with others and take their perspective, they will dislike having to criticise or discipline colleagues or subordinates.

## Thinking style

The next two factors relate to your preferred way of thinking.

*Factor 3: Tough-mindedness*
The factor Tough-mindedness reflects a practical, unsentimental orientation and is commonly seen in many managers.

**High scorers (Tough-minded)** are generally realistic, practical and conservative in their attitudes. Feelings and emotions (whether they are their own or others) will play little part in their life. They are inclined to reject the abstract in favour of more concrete and tangible solutions to problems. They generally prefer 'tried-and-tested' solutions to speculative experimentation and are often better at implementing ideas than generating them. Their unsentimental perspective can often be seen as hard and uncaring, particularly when associated with strong independence.

**Low scorers (Sentimental)** live in the world of ideas, are intellectually orientated and enjoy situations where they have the freedom to approach problems in new and innovative ways. Generally interested in artistic expression, believing that Art enriches life, they will have a sense of aesthetics and will appreciate good design.

*Factor 4: Control*
This dimension reflects the extent to which individuals have been affected by the moral values and rules of their environment and the degree of control they like to exercise over their lives.

**High scorers (Conforming)** are generally conservative and conscious of standards of behaviour. They are most comfortable dealing with the familiar and tend to stick to 'tried-and-tested' methods. This practical, low-risk approach to life tends to be linked to a high level of self discipline. They often display behaviour that is highly structured, reflecting a rigid adherence to high standards. They will have a strong sense of right and wrong and will rigorously attempt to maintain their standards. Although they are often skilled at applying technical skills, they will generally not see themselves as particularly creative.

Conforming people like to be in control of their lives and at work tend to defend the traditional way of doing things. They place a high value on integrity, standards and setting a good example. On the other hand, they are also often seen as being particularly resistant to new ideas and change. In some circumstances, they can be seen as inflexible and obstructive. They will be happiest in jobs that are stable with clear rules and an established routine.

**Low scorers (Open)**, in contrast, are more open-minded people who like to experiment. They are always on the lookout for new approaches, find it easier to ignore social rules and often view themselves as lacking the necessary self-discipline and persistence to see tedious tasks through to completion. They are tolerant and open in their attitudes, believing in the expression 'Live and let live'. On the other hand, they may reject tradition just for the sake of it and in so doing ignore perfectly good ways of doing things. Although they are creative, they can sometimes be criticised for being too impractical.

In the workplace, creative people embrace new opportunities and promote innovation. Although their enthusiasm is obvious, at times they will seem to be inconsistent or unreliable. Also their desire to be different can put them at odds with others. This may lead to problems in gaining promotion. They may also be inclined to take too many risks.

## Emotional style

*Factor 5: Confidence*

Finally the last factor, Confidence, is often referred to as Temperamentality, Anxiety or Neuroticism.

The evidence supporting the importance of the Anxiety personality factor in determining success at work is impressive.

**High scorers (Anxious)** admit to a variety of problems in coping with day-to-day situations. They are often rather tense and anxious, worried about what others think and deeply affected by circumstances. They are concerned about the future and often dissatisfied with their past achievements. Having been let down by others in the past may have taught them to be suspicious of the motives and abilities of other people.

**Low scorers (Confident)** describe themselves as calm, composed and satisfied with their life and their ability to cope with its daily challenges. They are relaxed and assertive individuals, who know their own minds and are comfortable with themselves. Optimistic and positive, they find it easier to deal with criticism constructively.

## What to do with the results

The questionaire results are only a snapshot of your personality. They do not mean that you necessarily behave in the way described above, or more importantly that you only behave just in one way. If, like most people, you occupy the middle ground between the two extremes, sometimes you will behave in one way, sometimes in another.

Nevertheless, from time to time most of us feel we would like to widen our behavioural repertoire and we often show this by admiring the qualities we see in others. If you examine the tables below, you may be able to identify things you admire in others or areas where you would like to improve. Some development activities are suggested under each headings. Your responses should also confirm the results of the questionnaire to some extent.

| Introvert | Extravert |
|---|---|
| I would really like to be a bit more outgoing. | I would like to be more self-aware. |
| I really admire their confidence. | I'm a bit lost if I don't have people around me. |
| *Activities* | *Activities* |
| Use more statements beginning with 'I think, I want . . .' | Spend more time thinking about yourself. |
| Ask people what they think. | Get more feedback. |
| Make more presentations, go to more functions, watch others. | Look at the more extreme reactions others show towards you. |

| Group-orientated | Independent |
|---|---|
| I really admire their drive and determination. | I wish I felt more part of the group. |
| | I think I should participate more. |
| *Activities* | *Activities* |
| Spend more time on your personal agendas. | Talk to people more. |
| Watch people more and practice their skills. | Practice listening skills, take up counselling. |
| | Force yourself to participate more. |

| Sentimental | Tough-minded |
|---|---|
| Sometimes I think I take things too much to heart. | I would like to be more creative. |
| I would like to be less sensitive. | I think I am too hard on others and unreceptive. |
| I wish I could be good at more practical things. | I really don't understand these strategic planning guys. |
| *Activities* | *Activities* |
| Analyse your feelings constructively. | Practice your listening skills. |
| | Learn new techniques for creativity. |
| Prove you can do practical things. | Put yourself into situations where you |
| Try to appreciate a more practical approach to life. | need to think more creatively or in an abstract way. |
| | Take up some new hobbies or interests. |

| Open | Conforming |
|---|---|
| I would like to be more organised, to plan things better. I always seem to leave things to the last moment. I admire their integrity and standards. | I think I am sometimes too much of a perfectionist. Sometimes I feel I may be 'stuck in a rut'. I hate change. |
| *Activities* Learn new organisation, planning or time management skills. Find out more about how others perceive your actions. | *Activities* Try reducing your standards at work. Put yourself in a situation where you cannot rely on your professional expertise. Try to do things more impulsively. |

| Confident | Anxious |
|---|---|
| Sometimes I think I am too relaxed. Some people think I don't really care. I would like to motivate myself more. | I'm too stressed out. I wish I could feel less anxious. I lose my temper too easily. |
| *Activities* Find things to do which excite you more. Talk to people more about what matters to you. Learn to lose your temper or patience more, or at least to send messages to others. | *Activities* Apply relaxation or stress management techniques. Constructively review the effect of not doing things or missing deadlines. Get better feedback. |

These are just a few suggestions to get you started. You should be able to identify many other ways of developing yourself.

# Summary

In this chapter, we have provided you with a simple questionnaire that assesses your stated preferences against five factors or dimensions as follows:

- Extraversion
- Independence
- Tough-mindedness
- Control
- Confidence

We have provided you with a simple summary of each of these factors and identified ways in which you can develop your behavioural skills to balance your natural preferences.

In the next chapter, we shall provide you with more detailed guidance on how to develop your personal skills and create effective action plans.

# Where to go next

So far, we have covered quite a lot. You have looked at the nature of personality, the way in which tests are designed, some of the main personality questionnaires and the way in which they are applied. In the last chapter, you should have completed a simple questionnaire to gain more insight into your own profile.

In this chapter, we shall examine how to apply this knowledge to your personal development. You will find the results of your questionnaire from the last chapter useful.

## Mastering your personality

The sheer volume of books on improving your personal effectiveness or achieving success is probably a reflection of just how difficult people find it to change personal attitudes and habits, just as the number of time management courses and devices to quit smoking reflects people's problems in these two areas.

The difficulty people experience in making changes to their personal behaviour is that it all sounds easy, but the practice is difficult. In the UK, at least, managers find it much easier to deal with practical outcomes, which is why nearly all the competence frameworks designed to support the Vocational Qualification framework (VQs) are based on functional skills (eg manage the budget, introduce quality systems). Although these skills are underpinned by critical elements of personal behaviour, most trainers and developers find they need to work hard to change these aspects of work-based behaviour significantly.

Changing from a bad habit, such as smoking or gambling, to a good one, such as a healthy diet or fitness regime, can serve as a good example of the success factors involved. To change your behaviour, you need to remember the following:

- It takes time and patience to achieve significant alterations in your behaviour.
- You need all the help you can get.
- You have to want to change.
- At the heart of your behaviour lie your basic beliefs and values. Once these change, everything else follows. Unlike practical skills, these values can be changed overnight, although this happens rarely.

In the last chapter, you may have identified ways in which you would like to develop your personality. Of course, we can all produce a long list of wishes like 'I wish I were more outgoing, assertive, creative, aware of the needs of others ...', just like a New Year's resolution list, but unless we can turn these into action plans, chances are they will just disappear and be forgotten in time.

To convert self-knowledge of your personality into action and success, you need to do three things:

- Raise your level of awareness.
- Identify your key development needs.
- Create realistic action plans.

## Raising your awareness

How often have you discovered something about your

performance at work too late to really do anything about it? The world is littered with examples of organisations badly damaged by personal effectiveness issues that were not dealt with – the CEO or the marketing director who were poor communicators, the financial director who took unacceptable risks etc. Yet it is all too common to find that when key staff are confronted with issues about their personal effectiveness, their response is 'I always suspected that, I wish someone had spoken to me about it earlier'.

Just as common, and a significant barrier to individual and organisational success, is a lack of awareness about what people admire you for. Often our reticence to seek feedback is cultural – we feel it's not quite right. But we should always remember that it's difficult to make changes unless we have a very good idea of how others see us. Here is some guidance on how to improve your self awareness.

*Increase your sources of feedback*
Frequent and regular feedback is the only way to increase your awareness of your personality effectively. Look for different sources – self-assessment tools, your colleagues, your boss, your partner and friends, even customers. Find ways of asking them what they think.

*Create your own map*
You should have noticed by now all of the commonly used personality questionnaires tend to be based on similar frameworks for personality factors. The only problem is that they use a language that is not yours. Try to develop your own model and understanding of how your personality works. You will find this gives you much more control over your life.

# Identifying development needs

In the last chapter, we suggested ways in which you could identify ways of improving your personal effectiveness. Here is some more guidance.

*Map your job and environment onto your profile*
In Chapter 4, we explained the relationship between job and person specifications and the use of personality questionnaires. In just the same way, you can review your current job, previous career and the effect of your environment on you to gain more insight into your personality.

*How well do you suit your current job? Which aspects delight you and which do you find frustrating? Are you moulding your career to suit your personal preferences and to develop them, or is your career changing you? How separate is your home and social life from the workplace? How different are you outside of work? Do you have regrets, things you want to do still? Why?*

*What is your ideal job? What is the environment like? Who would be your colleagues? How would you work? Why?*

These are dangerous questions to some people, usually because they feel anxious about the answers and don't want to 'take the lid off'. They are also liberating questions and critical to keeping your life in your hands.

*Map your aspirations onto your profile*
Only by identifying what you want out of life, can you begin to match these aspirations to your personality and to identify future action points. Senior managers are particularly prone to ignoring this aspect of their lives; after all, they have reached the top and can't really afford to change direction at this stage.

## Creating a realistic action plan

Assuming that you wish to develop your career, you should use any feedback or self-knowledge to identify priorities for development and an action plan for the future. This is, of course, the difficult part. Here are some general guidelines for developing your action plan.

- **Add the insight from this book to your overall assessment of your potential.**
  Map the trial questionnaire results against your own assessment and company appraisals. How do they link together? What key messages are there? What are your priorities for the future?

- **Gauge your readiness for improvement.**
  Just how ready are you to step out into the 'spot-light'? Do you need to acquire more general experience or to develop standard managerial skills and experience? What experience do you need to gain to give you the confidence to progress in this area?

- **Relate your development needs to your current job and career aspirations.**
  This may seem obvious, but always double-check your feelings and initial responses to feedback or guidance (such as appraisals) carefully. You may not want to change.

- **Link your action plans to your personal aspirations.**
  Unless your action plans link up with your core values and personal aspirations, you will find progress difficult. Explore these carefully and learn to review scenarios in your mind.

For example, what if you were asked to take on a different role or transfer to a new posting, possibly abroad? What is your immediate reaction? Even if you were keen to go, where would you like to go? Is there anywhere you wouldn't wish to go? Why? What does this tell you?

- *Focus on clear, manageable goals.*
- Don't take on too much at once.
- Look for short-term objectives with clear benefits for your career that fit longer term goals.
- Make your objectives SMART – Specific, Measurable, Achievable, Realistic and Time-constrained.

- *Look for models of best practice.*
- Look for people who embody the skills you admire.
- Build in opportunities to watch them at work or even better to work with them.
- Talk to them about how they think and how they acquired their skills.

- *Set up processes for on-going support and feedback.*
- Going it alone is always more difficult. Build your own support network, perhaps with colleagues who meet to discuss common problems.
- Make sure you get positive, constructive feedback. Negative, non-constructive feedback is to be avoided.
- Find ways of letting your colleagues and boss help you.
- Learn and master steps for increasing your awareness and self-control.
- Try to anticipate your 'hot-button' responses to situations where you do things inappropriately and try to prepare yourself to recognise these and take action.

- Find a colleague who will signal to you when you are doing something inappropriately.
- Recruit others to help you practice new skills.
- Actively seek out feedback on your performance. Don't wait for formal evaluations.

- *Choose your coaching support with care.*
  Everyone needs the support of their colleagues and organisation to maximise potential. Who is best suited to discuss the findings of personality assessments and to provide support in the future? Who will provide honest feedback to provide deeper insight into these findings? In reality, there may be several people who can help in this area, but one thing is certain – to develop your career you will need to enlist willing helpers who can teach you and coach you in new directions.

- *Expect setbacks.*
  When you begin your action plan, if progress seems too hard or slow, consider the possibility that you may be expecting too much from yourself or the organisation. Be more realistic. Allow for setbacks.

- *Build in your own rewards.*
  Success needs reward to sustain it. This simple fact is often overlooked. Find ways of rewarding yourself, even if it is only a special treat. Celebrate your successes.

- *Evaluate progress regularly.*
  Review, review and review! Be realistic and be prepared to adjust your plans if necessary.

## General comments on identifying development opportunities

One obvious way of developing your personal effectiveness skills is to attend suitable training programmes. There are, however, many other ways in which you can develop your skills without having to take time away from work or spend money. In trying to design an action plan for your future development, try to consider a range of in-house solutions that will broaden your practical experience and raise your profile. These might include:

- Using a mentor or coach within the organisation to identify development opportunities.
- Employing a greater variety of assessment tools to evaluate your skills effectively. Ask HR specialists for help in this area.
- Job shadowing, sharing or exchange schemes. These can be an effective way of learning how others do their work effectively.
- Special secondments to organisations or units that are centres of excellence for the skills you wish to develop.
- Participation in company-wide special projects to develop key initiatives.
- Self-help or action learning groups.

Above all, remember that effective managers possess broad management skills and can operate in a wide variety of situations. Try to avoid just concentrating on development within your professional area of expertise.

## And finally ...

Taking control of your personal development is a difficult but enormously rewarding task. You will find it more enlightening if you read round the subject and take the trouble to learn some of the latest techniques and tools available to assist this process. New personality tests are continually being created and may surprise you in the level of insight they are able to provide into the deepest aspects of your personality. Keep abreast of developments and good luck with your plans!

# Summary

Creating effective action plans to strengthen our personal effectiveness is not easy. Long-term success in this area requires you to:

- raise your level of awareness;
- identify your key development needs;
- create realistic action plans; and
- review your plans constantly and keep abreast of the latest developments.

# Resources

## Useful addresses

The British Psychological Society (BPS), 48 Princess Road East, Leicester LE1 7DR. Tel: (0116) 254 9568. Fax: (0116) 247 0787.

The Institute of Management (IM), Management House, Cottingham Road, Corby, Northants, NN17 1TT. Tel: (01536) 204222.

The Institute of Personnel and Development (IPD), IPD House, Camp Road, London, SW19 4UX. Tel: (020) 8971 9000.

## Test Suppliers and Publishers

Assessment for Selection and Employment, Darville House, 2 Oxford Road East, Windsor, Berkshire, SL4 1DF. Tel: (01753) 850333.

Oxford Psychologists Press Ltd, Lambourne House, 311–321 Banbury Road, Oxford, OX2 7JH. Tel: (01865) 311353.

The Psychological Corporation, Harcourt UK Ltd, 24–28 Oval Road, London NW1 7DX. Tel: (020) 7267446. Fax: (020) 7485 4752.

Psytech International Ltd, The Grange, Church Road, Pulloxhill, Bedfordshire, MK45 5HE. Tel: (01525) 720003.

Saville & Holdsworth Ltd, 3 AC Court, High Street, Thames Ditton, Surrey, KT7 0SR. Tel: (020) 8398 4170.

The Test Agency, Cray House, Woodlands Road, Henley-on-Thames, Oxon, RG9 4AE. Tel: (01491) 413413.

## Further reading

BPS, *Psychological Testing: Guidance for the User* (1989), BPS, Leicester.

Cattell, R B, *The Scientific use of factor analysis in behavioural and life sciences* (1978), Plenum Press, New York.

Cattell, R B, *The scientific analysis of personality* (1965), Penguin, Baltimore.

Equal Opportunities Commission, *Avoiding Sex Bias in Selection Testing: Guidance for employers* (1988), Manchester.

Eysenck, H J and Eysenck, S B G, *Personality Structure and Measurement* (1969), RKP, London.

Gael, S, *The Job Analysis Handbook for Business, Industry and Government* (1987), John Wiley and Sons.

Gordon, L V, *Manual for the Survey of Interpersonal Values* (1985), Science Research Associates, Henley.

IPD, *The IPM Code on Psychological Testing* (1993), IPD, Wimbledon.

Kline, P, *Personality: The Psychometric View* (1993), Routledge, London.

Pearn, M and Kandola, R, *Job Analysis: A Practical Guide for Managers* (1988), IPM.

Smith, M and Robertson, I, *Advances in Selection and Assessment* (1993), John Wiley and Sons.